A Question A Day

One Year Memory Journal for You and Your Dog

Written, illustrated, and created by Lauren Weatherly
PupperScouts.com
@PupperScouts

A Question A Day: One Year Memory Journal for You and Your Dog
Copyright 2024, Pupper Scouts ©, All rights reserved
Written, illustrated, and created by Lauren Weatherly

We would love to see photos or anecdotes depicting how you use this book!

-Tag us on social media: @Pupperscouts
-Visit our website: PupperScouts.com
-Send us an email: pupperscouts@gmail.com

ISBN: 979-8-9908069-1-7

No part of this book may be reproduced, copied, or transmitted in any form, or by any means including: photocopying, transcribing, etc., without written permission from the author.

2024 Pupper Scouts

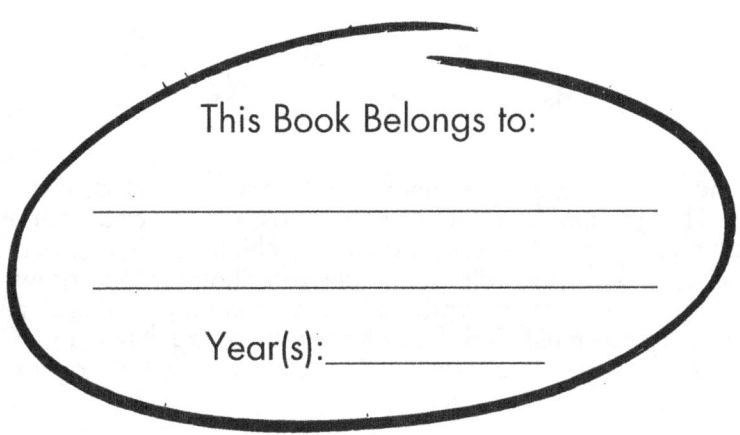

This Book Belongs to:
_____
_____
Year(s):_____

A Message from Lauren

From the very youngest age, my fondest memories include two things: 1) Exploring the nooks and crannies, broad canopies and dense underbrush of the forest behind my childhood home, and 2. Snuggling and playing with our family dog Shammy. As I grew, my exploration of the natural world expanded, and my relationship with furry friends multiplied. So naturally, as an adult living in Colorado, I merged these two passions into a life full of dog-friendly adventures.

Exploring wild places near and far with my two sweet puppers, Bonnie & Ada, is my most beloved activity. This is how Pupper Scouts was born! I started a silly little social media account to document and share our adventures in the wild. It was a form of journaling, but also a way to share our favorite hikes and adventures, as well as tips and tricks for traveling and adventuring. I had no idea it would take off the way it has, and it has enabled me to connect with others who cherish dog-friendly adventures as much as we do.

I have also found so much joy through journaling in a more traditional sense. Journaling has never come naturally to me, but I've pushed myself to explore the art form. Magically, the more I began writing down bits and pieces of what inspires me, what I notice, and what my pups experience, the more precious those experiences become. But my journals serve as more than just memories. They inspire future actions like adventure planning and goal setting, and they also nurture my creative mind by allowing me to play with words and dabble in sketching.

However, I find many journals to be too blank to get my brain going, or contain too many prompts to keep up with. So I set out to create something that was simple, but contained a little bit of guidance.

A Question A Day - A Memory Journal for You and Your Dog is the result! Inside, you'll find quick and easy prompts that enable you to define your own sense of adventure. Throughout, you will build your sense of connection with yourself, your dog, and your experiences together. We hope you enjoy it as much as we do!

ad·ven·ture
/əd'ven(t)SHər/
an exciting or remarkable experience

We invite you to challenge your own definition of adventure! Dogs are our best friends, our sweet companions, our fierce protectors, and our trusted confidantes. They love to explore the world just as much as we do - through sniffing, digging, splashing, rolling, running, sunbathing, and more. They deserve adventure, and we deserve to adventure with them! But adventure can mean so many things.

Not everyone has access to hiking right outside their door, but every landscape has fascinating places that can be explored with dogs. Not every dog can handle hiking in difficult terrain, but every dog owner enjoys getting out and about with their puppers in some way, shape, or form.

We believe that adventure can mean different things to different people and different pups. We think most important thing is to seek unusual, exciting, or unexpected experiences that bring you closer together.

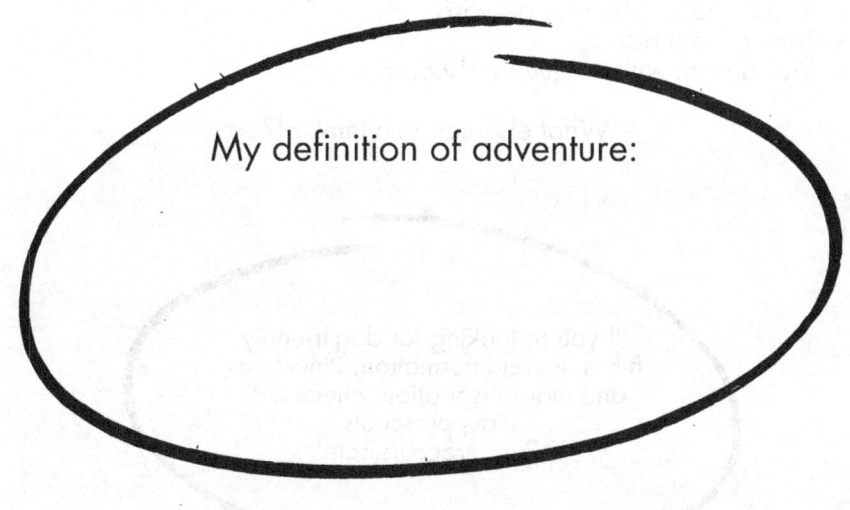

My definition of adventure:

Adventure Ideas

- Take a hike the woods, mountains, desert, beach, etc.
- Walk in a park near your home that you've never visited before
- Eat at a dog-friendly restaurant
- Play with a new toy in your own yard
- Attend a local festival or outdoor event that allows dogs
- Go for a walk or hike at nighttime and admire the stars
- Walk along a quiet dirt or gravel road in the country
- Go for a scenic drive and stop at some key points of interest to let your dog sniff around
- Learn a new trick
- Take your dog to visit a body of water where they can wade, splash, and/or swim
- Try out an agility course, or set one up in your yard or a local park
- Take your dog to a store that is dog-friendly to walk around
- Take a road trip to a near or far destination
- Go camping
- Walk in an urban landscape and look for street art
- Visit a new dog park
- Walk in an unfamiliar neighborhood
- Take your dog stand up paddleboarding at a lake near or far
- Walk in an urban sculpture or mural park
- Visit a friend with a large yard
- Take a boat ride
- Visit a park with unique landscaping

What else can you think of?

If you're looking for dog-friendly hikes, travel information, itineraries, and more inspiration, check out:
@pupperscouts
PupperScouts.com

January 1

What does adventuring with your dog mean to you?

_____
_____
_____
_____
_____
_____
_____

January 2

What is one adventure you want to have with your dog this month?

_____
_____
_____
_____
_____
_____
_____

January 3

What are 3 goals you have for your relationship with your dog this year?

_____
_____
_____
_____
_____
_____

January 4

What do you think your dog's new year's resolution is?

___
___
___
___
___
___

January 5

Where do you want to travel with your dog this year?

___
___
___
___
___
___
___

January 6

What drives you to be a better dog parent?

_____
_____
_____
_____
_____
_____
_____

January 7

My dog means a lot to me because ___

___
___
___
___
___
___

January 8

What are your dog's eyes saying to you right now?

___
___
___
___
___
___
___

January 9

Does your dog pick up on your emotions?

___
___
___
___
___
___

January 10

My dog is most peaceful when ___

_____
_____
_____
_____
_____
_____

January 11

When my dog looks at me, I feel ___

___
___
___
___
___
___

January 12

On a scale of 1 (laid back), to 10 (extra energetic), what would you rate your dog? Why?

_____
_____
_____
_____
_____
_____
_____

January 13

If your dog were a different animal, what would they be? Why?

January 14

How did your dog require your patience today?

___
___
___
___
___
___

January 15

The foundation of my relationship with my dog is ___

_____
_____
_____
_____
_____
_____
_____

January 16

How does your dog make you proud?

_____
_____
_____
_____
_____
_____

January 17

How do you make your dog proud?

___
___
___
___
___
___

January 18

If your dog could play an instrument, what would they play?

January 19

What could you do to make your dog feel more secure?

___
___
___
___
___
___
___

January 20

What was your dog born to do?

___
___
___
___
___

January 21

What time did your dog go to bed last night? What about you?

___

January 22

What song would you like to sing to your dog today?

___
___
___
___
___
___

January 23

My dog's favorite game is ___

_____
_____
_____
_____
_____
_____
_____

January 24

What is the sweetest thing your dog has done lately?

___
___
___
___
___
___
___

January 25

What is your dog an expert in?

___
___
___
___
___
___

January 26

What is your dog's most annoying habit?

___
___
___
___
___
___

January 27

I can always count on my dog to ___

_____
_____
_____
_____
_____
_____

January 28

True or False - A dog is the only thing on Earth that loves you more than they love themself.

___
___
___
___
___

January 29

How would your dog describe you?

___
___
___
___
___
___
___

January 30

Would you want your dog to live forever? Why?

January 31

If you could pick a theme song for your relationship with your dog, what would it be?

___
___
___
___
___
___
___

February 1

It is halfway between winter solstice and spring equinox. How will you celebrate with your dog?

_____
_____
_____
_____
_____
_____

February 2

What is one adventure you want to have with your dog this month?

___
___
___
___
___
___

February 3

What does your dog deserve today?

February 4

When I come home to my dog, I feel ___

_____
_____
_____
_____
_____

February 5

If you could change one thing about your dog, what would you change? Why?

_____
_____
_____
_____
_____
_____
_____

February 6

What do you hope never changes about your dog?

___
___
___
___
___
___

February 7

Three words I'd use to describe my dog are ___

February 8

The most recent development in my relationship with my dog is ___

_____
_____
_____
_____
_____
_____

February 9

If you had a million dollars to spend on your dog, what would you do with it?

_____
_____
_____
_____
_____
_____
_____

February 10

What life lesson has your dog taught you recently?

___
___
___
___
___
___

February 11

When did you last tell your dog you loved them?

___
___
___
___
___
___

February 12

Before I met my dog, I was ___

___
___
___
___
___
___

February 13

What are your goals as a dog owner?

_____
_____
_____
_____
_____
_____
_____

February 14

How many times have you thought about kissing your dog today?

_____
_____
_____
_____
_____
_____

February 15

How does your dog brighten your day?

___
___
___
___
___
___

February 16

How satisfying was your dog's day?
What about yours?

_____
_____
_____
_____
_____
_____

February 17

My dog and I are perfect companions because ___

___
___
___
___
___
___
___

February 18

Do you think your dog is an optimist or a pessimist?
Why?

February 19

What is your dog thinking in this exact moment?

___
___
___
___
___
___

February 20

Dedicate a song to your dog.

February 21

____ is really all that matters to my dog. ____ is all that matters to me.

February 22

What's next for you and your dog?

___
___
___
___
___
___

February 23

What kind of contest would you and your dog win together?

February 24

I always appreciate the way my dog ___

February 25

Describe one perfect day with your dog.

_____
_____
_____
_____
_____
_____

February 26

What has your dog been doing in the last 5 minutes?

February 27

It's ridiculously adorable when my dog ___

_____
_____
_____
_____
_____
_____

February 28

How do you deliver bad news to your dog?

February 29

Leap year bonus: Four years from now, what do you want to say to your dog?

_____
_____
_____
_____
_____
_____

March 1

How will you show your dog love today?

_____
_____
_____
_____
_____
_____
_____

March 2

What is one adventure you want to have with your dog this month?

_____
_____
_____
_____
_____
_____

March 3

What is one thing you want to tell your dog today?

___
___
___
___
___
___

March 4

Our favorite place to walk is ___. Why?

_____
_____
_____
_____
_____

March 5

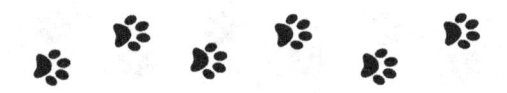

Does your dog need a sibling? Why or Why not?

___
___
___
___
___
___
___

March 6

My dog makes ___ look easy.

March 7

What is your dog's favorite treat?

___
___
___
___
___
___

March 8

What has your dog taught you about yourself lately?

March 9

What do you and your dog enjoy doing together?

_____
_____
_____
_____
_____
_____

March 10

It makes me laugh when my dog ___

_____
_____
_____
_____
_____
_____

March 11

What are 3 things you'd bring to a desert island with your dog?

___
___
___
___
___
___

March 12

What is the last thing you googled in relation to your dog?

___
___
___
___
___
___
___

March 13

If your dog could have one wish granted, what do you think they would wish for?

___

March 14

How did your dog make you laugh today?

_____
_____
_____
_____
_____
_____
_____

March 15

I appreciate when my dog ___

___
___
___
___
___
___

March 16

What is the best thing you bring to your relationship with your dog?

_____
_____
_____
_____
_____
_____

March 17

What makes you feel lucky as a dog parent?

___
___
___
___
___

March 18

What does your dog think is the best thing about you?

_____
_____
_____
_____
_____
_____
_____

March 19

What is your favorite time of day to play with your dog? What about your dog's favorite?

March 20

Spring is here! What do you like to do with your dog in the springtime?

_____
_____
_____
_____
_____
_____

March 21

If you made a toast to your dog, what would you say?

___
___
___
___
___
___

March 22

What offends your dog?

___
___
___
___
___
___
___

March 23

What are three things you have in common with your dog?

___
___
___
___
___
___

March 24

What positivity did your dog provide today?

_____
_____
_____
_____
_____
_____
_____

March 25

If your dog had a profession, what would it be?

___
___
___
___
___
___

March 26

If you had to describe your dog in a sigle word, what would it be?

March 27

If you could give your dog a superpower, what would it be? Why?

_____
_____
_____
_____
_____
_____

March 28

What is your dog's favorite new discovery?
What is yours?

___
___
___
___
___
___

March 29

What do you want to remember about your dog today?

___
___
___
___
___
___

March 30

The first line of the story of me and my dog is ___

_____
_____
_____
_____
_____
_____
_____

March 31

When was the last time you felt upset with your dog?

___
___
___
___
___
___
___

April 1

What will make your dog's tail wag today?

___
___
___
___
___
___

April 2

What is one adventure you want to have with your dog this month?

___
___
___
___
___
___
___

April 3

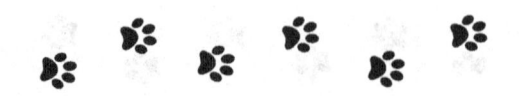

I worry about my dog when ___

_____
_____
_____
_____
_____
_____

April 4

What is your dog's favorite weather?

_____
_____
_____
_____
_____
_____

April 5

I wouldn't know anything about ___ if it weren't for my dog.

___
___
___
___
___
___
___

April 6

What does your dog need more of? What about you?

April 7

What do you think is your dog's ultimate dream come true?

April 8

If your dog were a superhero, what would they be called?

April 9

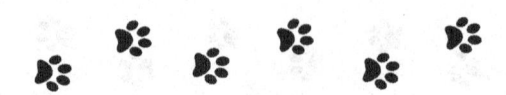

What's the very last thing you said to your dog?

___
___
___
___
___
___

April 10

What is your dog's most adorable habit?

April 11

It's been 100 days since the beginning of the new year. How are you doing on your goals?

___
___
___
___
___
___
___

April 12

It's been 101 days since the beginning of the new year. How's your dog doing on their resolution?

April 13

I'm so appreciative when my dog ___

April 14

Write a one-sentence poem about your dog.

April 15

What is one habit you wish your dog would break?

April 16

What's your perfect day with your dog?

___
___
___
___
___
___

April 17

How independent is your dog?

April 18

One of my best memories with my dog is ___

_____
_____
_____
_____
_____
_____

April 19

What is the last thing you bought for your dog?

April 20

What is your dog's favorite holiday?

_____
_____
_____
_____
_____
_____
_____

April 21

What is your dog scared of? What are you scared of?

___
___
___
___
___
___
___

April 22

If you had to guess, what is your dog thinking about right now?

April 23

What three things do you love most about your dog?

_____
_____
_____
_____
_____
_____

April 24

What motivates your dog? What motivates you?

April 25

How does your dog feel about other animals?

April 26

What is something you are willing to splurge on for your dog?

___
___
___
___
___
___

April 27

What makes you and your dog a great team?

_____
_____
_____
_____
_____
_____

April 28

Is your life with your dog a smooth ride, or an off-road adventure? Why?

_____
_____
_____
_____
_____
_____
_____

April 29

If you could use three words to describe your dog,
they would be ___

_____
_____
_____
_____
_____
_____
_____

April 30

When was the last time your dog shocked you?

May 1

It is halfway between spring equinox and summer solstice. How will you celebrate with your dog?

_____
_____
_____
_____
_____
_____

May 2

What is one adventure you want to have with your dog this month?

_____
_____
_____
_____
_____
_____

May 3

How will your dog make you giggle today?

May 4

If I could change my relationship with my dog,
I would ___

_____
_____
_____
_____
_____
_____

May 5

When I'm outside with my dog, I love to ___

_____
_____
_____
_____
_____
_____
_____

May 6

What are your top 3 wishes for your dog?

May 7

What do you believe is your dog's life purpose?
What is yours?

May 8

I'll never get tired of watching my dog ___

May 9

If your dog was a time traveler, what era would they be from?

_____
_____
_____
_____
_____
_____

May 10

What is the silliest thing you do with your dog?

_____
_____
_____
_____
_____
_____

May 11

What was the best moment of your dog's day?

May 12

I feel protective of my dog when ___

_____
_____
_____
_____
_____
_____
_____

May 13

What can't your dog live without?

May 14

If you had to sing a duet with your dog, what song would you choose?

May 15

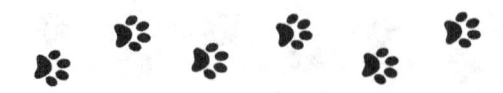

What has your dog been doing in the last 5 minutes?

___
___
___
___
___
___
___

May 16

What about your dog baffles you?

May 17

What is one thing about your dog that you hope never changes?

_____
_____
_____
_____
_____
_____

May 18

Is your dog brains, brawn, or beauty? Why?

May 19

What is your dog's favorite kind of adventure?

_____
_____
_____
_____
_____

May 20

What is the most rewarding aspect of your relationship with your dog?

May 21

What nicknames do you call your dog?

May 22

Does your dog know when you're happy/excited?
How do they react?

_____
_____
_____
_____
_____
_____

May 23

If you could do any one thing for an hour with your dog, what would it be?

May 24

The funniest part of my dog's body is ___

May 25

What celebrity does your dog resemble?

May 26

My dog gets distracted by ___

_____
_____
_____
_____
_____
_____

May 27

When I see my dog from across the room, I feel ___

_____
_____
_____
_____
_____
_____

May 28

When your dog sees you from across the room, what do they do?

_____
_____
_____
_____
_____
_____

May 29

What is your dog's greatest strength?

May 30

If you could get into your car and drive anywhere with your dog today, where would you go?

_____
_____
_____
_____
_____
_____
_____

May 31

When I see my dog wag their tail, I feel ___

_____
_____
_____
_____
_____
_____

June 1

How does your dog engage in self-care?
How do you?

___
___
___
___
___
___

June 2

What is one adventure you want to have with your dog this month?

___
___
___
___
___
___

June 3

What can you watch your dog do over and over?

June 4

What is your dog's grossest habit?

___
___
___
___
___
___

June 5

What kind of dog parent do you aspire to be?

June 6

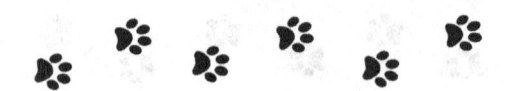

What kind of dog parent does your dog want you to be?

_____
_____
_____
_____
_____
_____

June 7

What do you think your dog is thankful for?

_____
_____
_____
_____
_____
_____
_____

June 8

Describe your love for your dog.

___

June 9

What celebrity would your dog enjoy spending time with?

June 10

Write down three words that describe today with your dog.

_____
_____
_____
_____
_____
_____

June 11

What do you think your dog wants more than anything? What about you?

June 12

What is your dog's perfect day?

___
___
___
___
___
___

June 13

If your dog was in a band, what would it be called?

_____
_____
_____
_____
_____
_____

June 14

What matters more than ever to your dog? To you?

_____
_____
_____
_____
_____
_____

June 15

Cuddling with my dog is like ___

_____
_____
_____
_____
_____
_____

June 16

What are you planning to do with your dog next weekend?

June 17

How has your dog grown this past year? How have you grown?

___

June 18

if you could choose one thing to do differently with your dog today, what would it be?

June 19

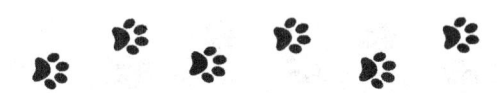

If your dog could call someone right now, who would they call?

___
___
___
___
___
___

June 20

Summer is here! What do you like to do with your dog in the summertime?

_____
_____
_____
_____
_____

June 21

Write down three goals for your relationship with your dog in this second half of the year.

___
___
___
___
___
___
___

June 22

What could your dog teach a class on?

June 23

My dog looks adorable when ___

___
___
___
___
___
___

June 24

Write an inspiring mantra for your relationship with your dog.

June 25

What is the most playful thing your dog did today?

_____
_____
_____
_____
_____
_____

June 26

What does your dog look like while sleeping?

June 27

What initially attracted you to your dog?

June 28

Does your dog know when you're sick or sad? How do they react?

___
___
___
___
___
___
___

June 29

Describe a time when your dog made you angry.
Are you happy with your reaction?

_____
_____
_____
_____
_____
_____
_____

June 30

If you and your dog owned a sports team, what would you name it?

_____
_____
_____
_____
_____

July 1

How did your dog make you smile today?

_____
_____
_____
_____
_____
_____

July 2

What is one adventure you want to have with your dog this month?

_____
_____
_____
_____
_____
_____

July 3

When was the last time you dreamed about your dog?

July 4

How does your dog feel about social gatherings?
How about you?

July 5

If you played hooky to spend the day with your dog, what would you do?

_____
_____
_____
_____
_____
_____

July 6

Does your dog have a bedtime routine?

July 7

If you could start a business with your dog, what would it be?

July 8

How many times have you thought about your dog today?

_____
_____
_____
_____
_____
_____
_____

July 9

My dog helps me with ___

July 10

What aspect of your relationship with your dog needs work?

_____
_____
_____
_____
_____
_____

July 11

What activity do you wish you did with your dog more often?

___
___
___
___
___
___

July 12

What do you notice about your dog today?

___
___
___
___
___
___
___

July 13

What do you do with your dog when no one is watching?

July 14

How does your dog inspire you?

July 15

What traditions do you share with your dog?

_____
_____
_____
_____
_____
_____

July 16

What hopes and dreams do you have for your dog?

_____
_____
_____
_____
_____
_____
_____

July 17

What rules does your dog break?

July 18

Can you remember the last time your dog appeared in a dream?

July 19

What is the most frustrating thing about your dog?

_____
_____
_____
_____
_____
_____

July 20

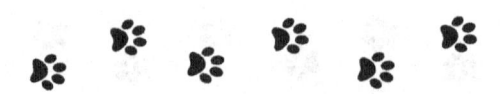

What does your dog need most? Why?

___
___
___
___
___
___
___

July 21

Where would you like to travel with your dog?

July 22

Do you think your dog is happy about the way your year is unfolding? Are you?

July 23

Do you spend more money on yourself or your dog?

___
___
___
___
___
___

July 24

I worry about my dog when ___

July 25

I am proud of my dog when ___

_____
_____
_____
_____
_____
_____

July 26

What award does your dog deserve to win?

_____
_____
_____
_____
_____
_____
_____

July 27

How did your dog make your life easier today?

July 28

My dog is the ___ of my life.

July 29

What's the foundation of your relationship with your dog?

___

July 30

I'm completely mesmerized by my dog when ___

_____
_____
_____
_____
_____
_____

July 31

Think back to when you first brought your dog home.
What has changed between then & now?

_____
_____
_____
_____
_____
_____

August 1

It is halfway between summer solstice and fall equinox. How will you celebrate with your dog?

_____
_____
_____
_____
_____
_____

August 2

What is one adventure you want to have with your dog this month?

_____
_____
_____
_____
_____
_____
_____

August 3

How did you make your dog smile today?

_____
_____
_____
_____
_____
_____

August 4

What part of your dog's body do you like the most?

August 5

What thoughts do you share only with your dog?

_____
_____
_____
_____
_____
_____

August 6

What is your dog's favorite place to visit?

_____
_____
_____
_____
_____

August 7

Which colors look best on your dog?

August 8

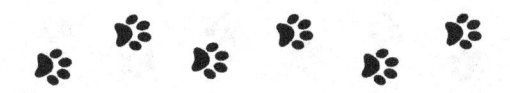

On what topic is your dog an expert?

August 9

My dog is at their best when ___

_____
_____
_____
_____
_____
_____

August 10

What is the biggest blessing in your dog's life?

___
___
___
___
___

August 11

What is your dog's favorite snack?

___
___
___
___
___
___

August 12

How do you and your dog have fun together?

August 13

What is your favorite outdoor activity to do with your dog?

August 14

What do you worry about related to your dog?

August 15

What is one thing that helps your relationship with your dog thrive?

___
___
___
___
___
___

August 16

Does your dog ever act wolfy?

August 17

What makes your dog feel safe?

___
___
___
___
___
___

August 18

My dog and I will always ___

_____
_____
_____
_____
_____
_____

August 19

What brings your dog joy?

August 20

Describe the last walk you enjoyed together with your dog.

_____
_____
_____
_____
_____
_____

August 21

Which of your friends do you think needs a dog?

August 22

What is your dog's weirdest habit?

August 23

What would your dog's news headline be today?

August 24

What musical genre fits your dog best? What about you?

August 25

Name a minor sacrifice you've made for your dog this year.

___

August 26

How many outfits does your dog own? What's missing from their wardrobe?

_____
_____
_____
_____
_____
_____
_____

August 27

What rituals with your dog make you happy?

August 28

What does your dog know about you that no one else does?

___
___
___
___
___
___

August 29

How did your dog's story begin?

August 30

If you could give your dog an award, what would it be?

___
___
___
___
___
___
___

August 31

If your dog could give you an award, what would it be?

September 1

What shenanigans did your dog get up to today?

September 2

What is one adventure you want to have with your dog this month?

_____
_____
_____
_____
_____
_____
_____

September 3

What song makes you think of your dog?

_____
_____
_____
_____
_____
_____
_____

September 4

What time did your dog wake up this morning?

September 5

What is the best thing about your dog?

_____
_____
_____
_____
_____
_____

September 6

If your dog had a catchphrase, what would it be?

_____
_____
_____
_____
_____

September 7

Is the weather outside today good for a walk with your dog?

September 8

What's the strangest thing your dog has ever done?

_____
_____
_____
_____
_____
_____
_____

September 9

How did you make your dog's life easier today?

___
___
___
___
___
___

September 10

What does your dog's inner puppy want? What about your inner child?

September 11

What is a minor challenge your dog is facing these days?

_____
_____
_____
_____
_____
_____

September 12

What do you think your dog daydreams about?

_____
_____
_____
_____
_____
_____

September 13

If your dog could play a human sport, what would it be?

_____
_____
_____
_____
_____
_____

September 14

What is your dog's most attractive quality?

September 15

What is your dog's most unattractive quality?

September 16

Does your dog follow their head or their heart?

September 17

What would you like to do more with your dog?

_____
_____
_____
_____
_____
_____

September 18

Who likes people more - You or your dog?

September 19

What is one thing you like to do for your dog?

September 20

What is your dog's strongest desire?

_____
_____
_____
_____
_____
_____
_____

September 21

Autumn is here! What do you like to do with your dog in the fall?

___
___
___
___
___
___

September 22

What is your favorite time of day to walk your dog?

September 23

Does your dog ever scare you?

September 24

If your dog could wake up tomorrow gaining one ability, what would it be?

_____
_____
_____
_____
_____
_____
_____

September 25

When is the last time your dog made you laugh out loud?

___
___
___
___
___
___

September 26

Being with my dog feels like ___

_____
_____
_____
_____
_____
_____

September 27

What reminds you of how much you love your dog?

September 28

If you were given $100 to spend on your dog today, what would you do with it?

September 29

When I hear my dog bark I feel ___

___
___
___
___
___
___

September 30

What non-canine animal is your dog most like?

October 1

What can you do to be a better friend to your dog?

October 2

What is one adventure you want to have with your dog this month?

October 3

If I were a poet, I'd compare my dog to ___

October 4

Where is one place you dream about being able to take your dog?

October 5

What would you rather not know regarding your dog?

October 6

What is your dog's guilty pleasure?

October 7

What have you told your closest friend about your dog?

___
___
___
___
___
___

October 8

How do you celebrate your dog's birthday?

October 9

What would you include in a time capsule about your relationship with your dog?

_____
_____
_____
_____
_____
_____
_____

October 10

When was the last time your dog got in trouble?

___

October 11

What is the most lovable thing about your dog?

October 12

What do you wish you were better at regarding your dog?

October 13

What do you and your dog disagree on?

October 14

How do you balance the needs for "me time" and "me-and-dog time"?

_____
_____
_____
_____
_____
_____
_____

October 15

What do you fear most about your dog getting older?

___
___
___
___
___
___
___

October 16

If your dog lived in a different era, which would it be?

_____
_____
_____
_____
_____
_____
_____

October 17

What do you do when you're upset with your dog?

___
___
___
___
___
___
___

October 18

How did your dog bring you happiness today?

_____
_____
_____
_____
_____
_____

October 19

If you made a playlist for your dog, what would the title be?

October 20

I wouldn't be surprised if my dog started ___

October 21

What new activity would you like to try with your dog?

___
___
___
___
___
___
___

October 22

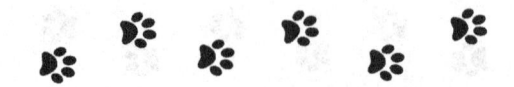

True or False - Dogs do speak, but only to those who know how to listen. Why?

___
___
___
___
___
___

October 23

What would make your dog happier?

October 24

What would make you happier as a dog parent?

_____
_____
_____
_____
_____
_____
_____

October 25

What was the very last thought to cross your dog's mind? What about yours?

_____
_____
_____
_____
_____
_____

October 26

What's the prevailing theme of your dog's life?
What about yours?

October 27

What's on your dog's to-do list?

October 28

What are 3 things your dog can't live without?

October 29

What's your favorite thing to do with your dog on a Sunday morning?

October 30

What was the last treat you bought for your dog?
What about for yourself?

October 31

Does your dog prefer tricks or treats? Why?

_____
_____
_____
_____
_____
_____

November 1

It is halfway between fall equinox and winter solstice.
What will you do to celebrate with your dog?

_____
_____
_____
_____
_____
_____
_____

November 2

What is one adventure you want to have with your dog this month?

___
___
___
___
___
___

November 3

If your dog were running for president, what would their slogan be?

___
___
___
___
___
___
___

November 4

What experience with your dog would you want to relive?

_____
_____
_____
_____
_____
_____

November 5

What's the most spontaneous thing you've done with your dog?

November 6

What was the last photo you took of your dog?

___

November 7

If your dog could have anything they wanted for dinner, what would it be? What about you?

November 8

What is your favorite holiday to celebrate with your dog?

November 9

If your dog could write a one sentence poem about you, what would it be?

November 10

My dog reminds me that ___

___
___
___
___
___

November 11

What do you find irresistable about your dog?

November 12

What's the next adventure you plan to take with your dog?

___
___
___
___
___
___

November 13

If I wrote a story about my dog, the first line would be ___

_____
_____
_____
_____
_____
_____
_____
_____

November 14

If I could fly anywhere with my dog, we'd go ___

_____
_____
_____
_____
_____
_____

November 15

Loving my dog is ___

_____
_____
_____
_____
_____
_____

November 16

What is something you hope your dog never does again?

November 17

Describe one thing your dog does that makes you feel loved?

___
___
___
___
___
___

November 18

If your dog went to human school, what would their best subject be?

___
___
___
___
___
___

November 19

If you and your dog both had a year to live, what would you do?

November 20

What imperfection do you find endearing in your dog?

___
___
___
___
___
___

November 21

I'd be completely shocked if my dog ___

___
___
___
___
___
___
___

November 22

If you could do anything with your dog today, what would it be?

_____
_____
_____
_____
_____
_____

November 23

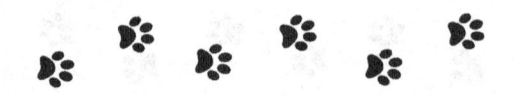

What is your dog doing in this exact moment?

___

November 24

What is the last text message you sent in which you mention your dog?

_____
_____
_____
_____
_____
_____
_____

November 25

What are you the most thankful for about your dog?

___
___
___
___
___
___
___

November 26

What is one thing you're grateful for? What is your dog grateful for?

November 27

What is the first word that comes to mind when you think of your dog?

___
___
___
___
___
___
___

November 28

What is the biggest lesson your dog has learned this year? What about you?

November 29

When is the last time your dog felt misunderstood?

November 30

What would be the title of your dog's autobiography?

___
___
___
___
___
___

December 1

How are you and your dog alike?

December 2

What is one adventure you want to have with your dog this month?

_____
_____
_____
_____
_____
_____

December 3

I like to brag about the fact that my dog ___

December 4

What is one treasured memory of you and your dog in the past year?

_____
_____
_____
_____
_____
_____

December 5

What holiday song makes you think of your dog?

_____
_____
_____
_____
_____
_____

December 6

What is the fist sentence of your dog's memior?

_____
_____
_____
_____
_____
_____

December 7

What lights up your dog's life? What about yours?

___
___
___
___
___
___
___

December 8

When I see my dog's tail wag, I feel ___

_____
_____
_____
_____
_____
_____

December 9

Does your dog like cold weather? Why or why not?

December 10

What's on your dog's wish list?

December 11

If your dog were to go missing, where would you look for them?

___
___
___
___
___
___

December 12

Is there anything you need to apologize to your dog for?

December 13

What is the first thing you said to your dog today?

___

December 14

If your dog could google something right now, what would it be?

December 15

What's your secret to a great relationship with your dog?

_____
_____
_____
_____
_____
_____

December 16

What would your dog's theme song be called?

December 17

What's the cutest thing your dog did this week?

_____
_____
_____
_____
_____

December 18

Is anything missing in your dog's life? What about yours?

_____
_____
_____
_____
_____
_____
_____

December 19

When was the last time your dog shocked you?

December 20

What friends/family members love your dog most?

___
___
___
___
___
___
___

December 21

Winter is here! What do you like to do with your dog in the wintertime?

_____
_____
_____
_____
_____
_____

December 22

How has your dog's life changed this year?

___
___
___
___
___
___
___

December 23

What calms your dog down? What about you?

_____
_____
_____
_____
_____
_____

December 24

How were your dog's choices today? How about yours?

___

December 25

If you could give your dog a wildly extravagant gift, what would it be?

___
___
___
___
___
___
___

December 26

What have you realized about your dog in the last year?

December 27

What is the worst thing that happened to your dog this year?

_____
_____
_____
_____
_____
_____

December 28

What have you learned in the last year about your relationship with your dog?

___
___
___
___
___
___

December 29

What is one thing you wish for your life with your dog next year?

___
___
___
___
___
___

December 30

What is your favorite day with your dog from the past year?

_____
_____
_____
_____
_____
_____

December 31

Describe your future with your dog.

_____
_____
_____
_____
_____
_____
_____

Made in the USA
Monee, IL
22 October 2024